GOD AND POLITICS

Mark Dever has provided an insightful exposition of what it means for us to 'render unto Caesar what is Caesar's,' casting a positive vision for Christian engagement in politics. Highly recommended.

SAM ALLBERRY, AUTHOR OF *IS GOD ANTI-GAY?*

There's no one I trust more than Mark Dever to teach what the Bible tells us about Christianity and government. I commend this book to you.

COLLIN HANSEN, THE GOSPEL COALITION

This is a little book full of big surprises. There are many books about God and politics but few that are all about Jesus and very few that are about one verse in the Bible. Mark Dever superbly unpacks Jesus' surprising response to his opponents question, which Jeremy Paxman would have been proud of – is it right to pay taxes to Caesar or not? He has become every politician's favourite author by daring to thank us for 'doing God's work'. But Mark does not let you or me get away with just giving 'that coin back to Caesar' given his clarion call to 'give yourself to God'. He sets out Jesus' wonderful vision which goes deeper and higher than politics. It leads us to grow in our respect for politics and our hope for better to come.

DAVID BURROWES, MEMBER OF PARLIAMENT, UK

GOD AND POLITICS

JESUS' VISION FOR SOCIETY, STATE AND GOVERNMENT

MARK DEVER

10 Publishing
a division of **10** of those.com

Copyright © 2016 by Mark Dever
First published in Great Britain in 2016

The right of Mark Dever to be identified as the Author of this Work has been asserted by him in accordance with the Copyright, Designs and Patents Act 1988.

British Library Cataloguing in Publication Data
A record for this book is available from the British Library

ISBN: 978-1-910587-43-0
Designed by Diane Warnes
Printed in the UK by CPI

10Publishing, a division of 10ofthose.com
Unit C, Tomlinson Road, Leyland, PR25 2DY, England
97 Karago Ave, Suite 5, Youngstown, OH 44512, USA
Email: info@10ofthose.com
Website: www.10ofthose.com

NO VISION?

"That's the problem with Christianity," my friend told me. "You have no vision for the state, for society as a whole." He was a Muslim but had become a good friend. I remember where we were when we had this conversation. I had had others like it before but not with as good a friend as this man had become. He had been a guest in our home recently and as we were talking together he expressed how thankful he was that my wife and I were trying to raise our children to be 'holy', as he put it. We both commiserated about the moral state of late twentieth century Britain where we then lived. And then he said this, 'That's the problem with Christianity. You have no vision for the state, for society as a whole.'

Is he right? Does Christianity have a vision for the state or for society as a whole or is Christianity, as my friend implied, so heavenly minded that it is of no earthly good? This difference between Christianity and Islam has often been noted.

Marx and Freud thought that Christianity had a pacifying escapism. Later Communists had been more suspect of its revolutionary implications. Some rulers have condemned it as treasonous while others have found Christians to be useful dupes. In the name of Christ some people have withdrawn into lives of hermits or monasteries or Amish enclaves.

In the name of Christ others have imagined their faith lived out in military crusades or in cleansing purges where those who are theologically wrong are burned to death, or where slavery is abolished, or abortion is opposed.

In the West and in our day, writers wonder about the impact of Christian faith on public life. David Brooks wrote in *The New York Times* wondering if US Christian writers and preachers like David Platt signal a new spirit of responsibility and frugality and repentance for excess. Brooks notes that after times of boom in America, when bust follows, there are always creatures who come in and preach frugality.[i]

In the US, intellectuals speculate about the vanishing of Protestants and in the upper echelons of our legal community, politicos speculate on what the effect of the evangelical vote will be on the coming elections. In an increasingly multicultural setting in many countries, politicians wonder about the effect of religious groups on voting patterns. And older Christians simply wonder what has happened. They wonder what they have done in their own lifetimes that have caused things unthinkable in Eisenhower's America or Churchill's and Macmillan's Britain to now be the case.

TV quickly moved from appearing to support families to undermining them instead. Divorce and abortion have moved from being illegal to being inalienable rights. Births to married couples have become rarer, while illegitimacy and co-habitation, once unacceptable, are now the norm in many communities. Pornography floods our societies, and in our brave new world, it is more acceptable socially and legally for a man to have a husband than for someone to pray publicly in a school in the name of Jesus.

Is my Muslim friend right? Does this show us the problem that there is with Christianity? As Christians, those who recognize Jesus Christ as God Incarnate and who worship Him, what do we do? How does Jesus teach us to think about these matters? Let us consider that as we join Jesus in the last week of His earthly ministry.

JESUS ON
THE SCENE

I want to take you to Mark chapter 12 verses 13–17. But because of the seriousness of the topic, I am going to be quoting from all over the Bible to try to help give us a biblical theology in this area. Mark 12 verses 13–17 says:

13 Later they sent some of the Pharisees and Herodians to Jesus to catch him in his words. 14 They came to him and said, "Teacher, we know that you are a man of integrity. You aren't swayed by others, because you pay no attention to who they are; but you teach the way of God in accordance with the truth. Is it right to pay the imperial tax to Caesar or not? 15 Should we pay or shouldn't we?"

But Jesus knew their hypocrisy. "Why are you trying to trap me?" he asked. "Bring me a denarius and let me look at it." 16 They brought the coin, and he asked them, "Whose image is this? And whose inscription?"

"Caesar's," they replied.

17 Then Jesus said to them, "Give back to Caesar what is Caesar's and to God what is God's."

And they were amazed at him.

We see, after a ministry around the countryside in Galilee and beyond, that Jesus has now gone south to the capital of Judea, Jerusalem. It is a national week of religious celebration, their Passover. Thousands and thousands of pilgrims stream into Jerusalem bringing sacrifices. It is a kind of Christmas retail season for the folks of the temple. I mean, this is when all the big sales happen. It is the apex of the years, the zenith. It is into this important context that Jesus has come, raising the people's expectations and, with that, the potential for trouble.

He enters the city on a Sunday afternoon. We call it the "triumphal entry". He then goes to the temple, doesn't say anything and walks back out into the evening. He and His disciples, like most of the pilgrims, would stay outside the city. There weren't hotels. There wasn't room in Jerusalem for these thousands of pilgrims, so they would go out to one of the villages where they might have a relative or know someone, and would have arranged to stay there. Jesus and the disciples, each evening of this week would leave the city, walk down the valley, across to the Mount of Olives and stay in the nearby village of Bethesda.

Jesus goes back into Jerusalem on the Monday, and this time He creates a scene in the temple courts. He dramatically interrupts the commerce and He condemns the stewardship of the religious leaders as corrupt.

It is now the next day, Tuesday, which in Mark's Gospel covers chapter 11 verse 20 through the rest of chapters 11, 12 and 13. It is a long day of controversy and parables, as the priests were trying to trap Jesus. You see there in chapter 11 verse 27 that Jesus arrives on the Tuesday in the temple courts, these huge precincts outside the temple building itself, which were part of the temple complex. As soon as Jesus arrives a kind of executive committee of the ruling body, the Sanhedrin, publicly ask Jesus for His credentials. They want to know by what authority He had done what He had done the day before.

They were trying to trap Him, but He exposed their corrupt self-interest to the people and then he told the story or the parable you see in chapter 12 verses 1 to 12, in which Jesus clearly implies that God's Son has come, that He is God's Son and that He has come to reassert God's ownership over His people. But in this parable He prophesied that they would reject Him and they would kill Him and they would then in turn be judged by God. And you can see their response, in verse 12. "Then [they] looked for a way to arrest him because they knew he had spoken the parable against them. But they were afraid of the crowd; so they left him and went away."

VERBAL AMBUSH

But, though they went away, they figured out something else to do. In verse 13—17 it says, "Later they sent some of the Pharisees and Herodians to Jesus to catch him in his words. They came to him and said, 'Teacher, we know that you are a man of integrity. You aren't swayed by others, because you pay no attention to who they are; but you teach the way of God in accordance with the truth. Is it right to pay the imperial tax to Caesar or not? Should we pay or shouldn't we?' But Jesus knew their hypocrisy. 'Why are you trying to trap me?' he asked. 'Bring me a denarius and let me look at it.' They brought the coin, and he asked them, 'Whose image is this? And whose inscription?' 'Caesar's,' they replied. Then Jesus said to them,'Give back to Caesar what is Caesar's and to God what is God's.' And they were amazed at him."

You see the depth of the opposition that is evident as natural enemies join together. The Pharisees are the pro-populist Jewish party, the party of the people. They don't like the Roman rule. The Herodians are the servants of Herod, the puppet king that Rome put on the throne. They don't do anything together. But here they are. The freedom fighters and the collaborators working together. Now they are a "they". They are sent from the they of verse 12, which is the they of chapter 11 verse 27 (the chief priests, elders and teachers of the law), and they form this unlikely combination we read of in verse 13 to purposely catch Jesus. This was a premeditated verbal ambush. They conspired to deceive Him with flattery but, as it says in verse 15, "Jesus knew their hypocrisy." They came in malice to trap this man of truth. The religious game wardens had gone out hunting that day.

LYING TO THE TRUTH, IGNORING THE WAY, SEEKING TO KILL THE LIFE, SEEKING AS MARK SAYS, TO TRAP HIM.

Consider for a moment the dark irony of their mission; lying about the truth to the one who was the truth. Sinning against the holy one who made them in His image to bear His holy image. Seeking to kill the one who would be their only hope eternally. Lying to the truth, ignoring the way, seeking to kill the life, seeking as Mark says, to trap Him. They come dragging their bait behind them and throwing it out to Him, "a little question". They have worked on it. It is a very particular question, meant to glisten and attract this would-be Messiah. Have you ever been asked one of those questions that you didn't want to answer?

TO PAY OR
NOT TO PAY?

Here they asked that kind of question to Jesus. It was a good question for their purposes. "Is it right to pay the imperial tax to Caesar or not? Should we pay or shouldn't we?" This is not a kind of "Do you like taxes or not?" question. This is 100 times more emotionally charged than that. When you understand this setting, the tax that is referred to is the Roman imperial tax. Every adult male had to pay it; they used a denarius coin. It was about a day's wages. They paid it with this.

We actually get our word 'census' from the word for this tax. It is how they kept track of the population of the empire. It is how they funded the troops that occupied Jerusalem. One denarius for one male. It was hateful to the Jews. They could not stand this tax. Every single coin like that in circulation was a sign of their subjugation to the Roman Empire. Every single coin proclaimed that Caesar was their Lord now and it even claimed He was God on the coin. They hated that coin. They hated that tax. It was that tax back in AD 6 that had caused the revolt up in Galilee that the Romans had put down. It would be that same tax 60 years later that would cause yet another revolt, in AD 66, that the Romans would put down. Taxes are often associated with revolutions.

The Pharisees and Herodians were trying to either expose Jesus as a fraud, a pretend Messiah who had no plans to deliver Judea from Roman domination, or as a revolutionary, who was opposed to the tax and therefore liable to the full weight of Roman punishment. That was a very appropriate question to come from this unlikely assortment of pro-Roman Herodians and pro-Jewish Pharisees. It was a kind of heads I win, tails you lose question. No way around it. It was very clever. They made Jesus choose between the Romans or the people and whichever one He picks, He loses the other and His mission is sunk. They had done a good job on the question.

HE WOULD LOSE BY ANSWERING THIS QUESTION, EITHER HIS POPULARITY OR HIS LIFE.

He would lose by answering this question, either His popularity or His life.

But you know, even more amazing than their question was Jesus' answer. And that is what we want to give most of our time to. What does it mean for us to follow Jesus in this teaching? In what He says here? And does it have anything to do with that objection that my Muslim friend raised so many years ago now? Should Christians have a vision for society, for the state, for politics?

A PAGAN STATE IS A LEGITIMATE STATE

The first thing we should note from this is that Christians are good citizens, or at least we should be. We get this from the surprising first half of Jesus' answer there in verse 17 when He says "Give back to Caesar what is Caesar's". Now, I say surprising not because those words are surprising to most of us, they're not. Those are some of the most famous words of Jesus. But, I say surprising because at the time He spoke them they were unexpected. They were startling. This rabbi apparently trying to gain popularity in the temple precincts just endorsed using an idolatrous coin to pay a tax of the Roman oppressors. They were shocked at these words that Jesus speaks. He got out of the rhetorical checkmate that these leaders tried to put Him in.

But, too many readers admire Jesus' rhetorical dexterity and miss what it is that He is actually teaching. This is more than just a clever reply. In this short answer, Jesus establishes a biblical theology of government, and He applies it to the new phase in history of God's people that He was beginning. While it is going too far to say that Jesus' statement here established a wall of separation between church and state, or made the state secular; I think

Jesus' affirmation of paying taxes to the Roman government does show that even a pagan state is a legitimate state. That was an amazing thing for Him to say.

CHRISTIANS SHOULD BE GOOD CITIZENS

I remember once being asked to address the Libertarian Society at Cambridge on why society needs a state. I remember, as I researched and thought about it, I was impressed by what a deeply biblical thing human government is. Human government is not legitimate fundamentally because the government controls the army and the police. You know, "might makes right". Human government is not legitimate because of some social contract made somewhere back in the mythical, mystical mist of time.

Human government is not legitimate fundamentally because of an election – *vox populii vox dei*, the voice of the people is the voice of God.

Human government is not legitimate fundamentally because of a Marxist idea of inevitability, or merely for economic necessity or some psychological need we all have to be controlled.

Let's think for a moment about what the Bible teaches about government, and put Jesus' teaching here in the larger context of what God has revealed.

The story of the Bible begins with human history, and with that human history as soon as it begins in the very first chapter of the Bible, you find the story of government beginning. What we find is that human government reflects God's initial charge in Genesis 1 verse 28, "fill the earth and subdue it." It is the government of the earth that we are given at our very creation. Almost any government is better than anarchy. That is what we find again and again.

Now, take the Roman government of Jesus' day. It was abusive, even despised. However, the Roman government was still fulfilling the role of providing order and some measure of justice. Government does good by maintaining civil order and peace and providing a stage for us to obey God's commands to fill the earth and subdue it. To live as we read in 1 Timothy 2 verse 2 "peaceful and quiet lives in all godliness and holiness".

The Bible teaches us that God is sovereign over all and that the state is His servant. That is why Christians can usually obey it. Authority by its very nature reflects God.

AUTHORITY BY ITS VERY NATURE REFLECTS GOD.

King David's last words are true, "When one rules over people in righteousness, when he rules in the fear of God, he is like the light of morning at sunrise on a cloudless morning, like the brightness after rain that brings grass from the earth." (2 Samuel 23:3–4).

You see, this is why Proverbs can say in chapter 14 verse 34: "Righteousness exalts a nation, but sin condemns any people." So we are not surprised when the Lord Almighty told the Israelites in exile in Babylon, in Jeremiah 29 verse 7, "seek the peace and prosperity of the city to which I have carried you into exile. Pray to the LORD for it, because if it prospers, you too will prosper."

The purpose of all government should be to bless those within the scope of its authority. Not to use it for yourself if you are in government, but as Paul says in Romans 13 verse 4, "They are God's servants, agents of wrath to bring punishment on the wrongdoer."

All government has power only as God entrusts authority to them. So Jesus would say to Pilate, the Roman governor, just a couple of days later, "You would have no power over me if it were not given to you from above" (John 19:11). I am not saying that God thought the Roman rule of Judea was a great thing. Rather, He was sovereign over it for His own glory.

The longest single passage in scripture instructing us about how we Christians are to think about government is in Romans 13. You may not be aware that the Bible talks about things like this, but it does.

Let everyone be subject to the governing authorities, for there is no authority except that which God has established. The authorities that exist have been established by God. ² Consequently, whoever rebels against the authority is rebelling against what God has instituted, and those who do so will bring judgment on themselves. ³ For rulers hold no terror for those who do right, but for those who do wrong. Do you want to be free from fear of the one in authority? Then do what is right and you will be commended. ⁴ For the one in authority is God's servant for your good. But if you do wrong, be afraid, for rulers do not bear the sword for no reason. They are God's servants, agents of wrath to bring punishment on the wrongdoer. ⁵ Therefore, it is necessary to submit to the authorities, not only because of possible punishment but also as a matter of conscience.

⁶ This is also why you pay taxes, for the authorities are God's servants, who give their full time to governing. ⁷ Give to everyone what you owe them: If you owe taxes, pay taxes; if revenue, then revenue; if respect, then respect; if honor, then honor.

It is out of this kind of understanding of government that Paul will later write to Timothy in 1 Timothy 2 verse 2, when he writes telling him to pray for "kings and all those in authority, that we may live peaceful and quiet lives in all godliness and holiness".

It is why Peter writes in 1 Peter 2 verse 13–14,17, "Submit yourselves for the Lord's sake to every human authority: whether to the emperor, as the supreme authority, or to governors, who are sent by him to punish those who do wrong and to commend those who do right... Show proper respect to everyone, love the family of believers, fear God, honour the emperor."

CHRISTIANS ARE GOOD FOR A COUNTRY

As Christians, we believe that government is one of a number of enterprises that we can be involved in, that are not specifically Christian, but are good and even mediate the blessing of God to us. These things don't need to be Christian to be in some real sense good and something that blesses people.

> FOR ALL OUR SIN, I THINK THAT HISTORY SHOWS AGAIN AND AGAIN THAT CHRISTIANS ARE GOOD FOR A COUNTRY.

I wonder what your kind of political, social philosophy is? Do you think that unfettered self-interest is better to have as the basis of society? For all our sin, I think that history shows again and again that Christians are good for a country. All people are made in God's image. We are all made to display that image to each other, and Christians are called and enabled by God to live out that image, and to display love in a much fuller way than we could before we became Christians. As Christians, we are called to live a better, fuller life which should bring a blessing to those around us. The Bible supports the implication of Jesus' exhortation here to pay for even non-Christian governments, because by the nature of what they do, governments are made to be good, to reflect God's own authority.

Let me just do a very rare thing in the West and thank those of you who work for a government in any sense — those of you who work for the district or state governments or local governments, thank you! What you do in your job is in part reflecting God's own authority, as you keep order and peace and work for justice in our society. Thank you for the way you work to help display God's glory. You are doing God's work.

In fact, whatever sphere you are in, you are called to exercise the authority that you have as a reflection of God's own authority. All those in authority are to reflect and uphold the morality that God has created us all to have, in order to reflect his own character.

Even when governments support immorality and sin, as every government since the Fall has done in one way or another, we are at least normally to continue to support it. As we correct and improve it, we should be very slow to conclude that even when a particular sin is propagated that this removes the rightful authority of the government. We should be very slow to come to that conclusion. For Christians, this means that we are law-abiding, and tax-paying.

We do not cheat on our taxes. Christians are honest. We may or may not agree with the taxes, but if they are levied by proper authority, we pay them, as we should. We should be honest in it all and we should thank God for all the good there is in our government, establishing peace, protecting religious freedom, promoting justice. This means that we should be involved in encouraging good work in our government, and through its members.

Now, you will notice that many churches support Caesar by praying regularly, as we have just read in 1 Timothy verse 2, "for kings and all those in authority". We should pray for those in authority. Why would we do that? Because God's Word tells us to. You know, I have prayed for President Clinton and I have prayed for President Bush and now I am praying for President Obama and if I am here when the next President comes in, I will pray for him or her too. We should pray for those who are in authority over us. That is how we give to Caesar what is Caesar's, by working to improve life in our neighborhood and our district as God gives us opportunity, to preach and to display His gospel in our living. It is in our nature as Christians to be good citizens, but no earthly kingdom is to be identified as uniquely God's people.

CHRISTIANS ARE INTERNATIONAL

How do you get that out of "Render to Caesar the things that are Caesar's" (Mark 12:17, KJV) I will show you!

It is not complicated. Jesus' approval of paying taxes to Rome was revolutionary. By this Jesus shows us that the legitimacy of a government is not determined by whether it supports the worship of the one true God, or even allows for it.

By Jesus not requiring those who follow Him only to support states that are formally allied to the true God as Old Testament Israel had done, Jesus unhitches His followers from any particular nation. That is over and done now. If Christians can support Rome, what government could they not support? This is the government that killed Christ and almost all the apostles. And here Jesus is telling them, pay for it. Pay that tax that is going to pay the salary of the very men who are about to drive the nails into My hands, not because what they are doing is right, but because government reflects the character of God. God will deal with them.

We Christians are freed from supporting any one particular nation. We are freed to support whatever government there is for whatever land God has called us to live in. Jesus, then, is not putting Himself as a theonomist in the world. He is not saying you should take the Old Testament laws and legislate them in every nation on earth. Jesus is saying the opposite of that when He is saying "Give back to Caesar what is Caesar's".

Remember what he would say to Pilate in just a couple of days. John 18 verse 36: "My kingdom is not of this world." Now, Christ was bringing His kingdom into this world that would culminate in His return and His direct and personal rule, but until then, His people would be under the reign of all sorts of kings and emperors. Joseph and Daniel had been under other rulers in the Old Testament, just as Christ Himself was. All such reigns of earthly kings and nations would be temporary. But Christians are like cockroaches. We can survive anything by the grace of God. We are not dependent on just governments for the gospel going forward.

Think of fellow believers suffering in Pakistan. Our brothers and sisters in Pakistan should give to Caesar what is Caesar's. They should support their government. Again this means that God's people will not be building a single nation which alone will have legitimacy before God, the Christian country, but rather God's people will be international.

Jesus teaches here that His followers would not be like the Jewish state had been, nor like Rome or other pagan states had been, allied to the worship of a particular God. This was new, and a shocking thing to say. Ever since the days of Moses, God's people had been called into a national covenant with God. You can read the book of Exodus and on throughout Israel's history over 1,000 years and more to see this.

There is King David and the exile and the return, there is Ezra and Nehemiah. You see this throughout the Old Testament from God's instructions to His people uniquely in the Passover where they, the particular ethnic Jews, were to do a certain thing to be saved from the angel of death. Instructions He did not give to the majority population, the Egyptians. From its inception, all the way through to the Lord calling Israel at Sinai and promising them a special relationship with Him, God emphasized their special place. "Now if you obey me fully and keep my covenant, then out of all nations you will be my treasured possession. Although the whole earth is mine, you will be for me a kingdom of priests and a holy nation." (Exodus 19:5–6)

This is what God had called His people to be for a time, as their whole nation became a prophecy of what was to come in Christ. Israel lived out in a three-dimensional way what was to happen in Christ. It was a dim preview of the blessings of reconciliation that were to come between God and man. Now, we are an international people, not fundamentally a people of one ethnic group with promises running in one ethnic line. If you are not very familiar with Christianity, maybe all this about it being international surprises you. Christianity is international. The church of Jesus Christ today is international. It is spread all over the world. It has been historically. It has never been just an American thing or a Western thing. In fact, from its very earliest beginnings, the worship of the true God has always been something envisioned as being for all the nations.

ALL NATIONS

Back in Genesis, chapter 12 verse 3, when God first called Abram out of Ur of the Chaldeans, He made His promise to Abram, that "all peoples on earth will be blessed through you". Every time a Gentile joined the Old Testament people of God, this promise was foreshadowed. You could also see glimmers of the international nature of God's people in the examples of Joseph in Egypt and Daniel and others in exile, continuing to faithfully serve God even while they weren't in Israel.

It has always been a question for our Muslim friends, how can you be a Muslim outside of a Muslim nation? Because Islam is about submission, and submission to the rule. It has never been a question for Christians. We well understand in this fallen world that we are in exile no matter who is in charge. We have always lived as exiles and we will always live as exiles. We have no Mecca in this world.

It is here in the New Testament, though, right in this place in the ministry of Jesus that Jesus turns His followers to the nations. We read in Matthew 28:18–20 of Jesus' final instructions to His disciples, "All authority in heaven and on earth has been given to me. Therefore go and make disciples of all nations, baptizing them in the name of the Father and of the Son and of the Holy Spirit, and teaching them to obey everything I have commanded you."

And this is exactly what we see begin to happen at Pentecost as God's Spirit is poured out on people from various nations.

This is a story we follow through the book of Acts as we watch the gospel spread, first in Jerusalem and then to Samaria in Acts 8, and then to the Gentiles and Cornelius in Acts 10, and then throughout the Eastern Mediterranean. The book ends with Paul in Rome poised to take the gospel from what was then the sort of center of the world to every place.

That is exactly what God has been about and we know from the book of Revelation that God's international purpose for the church will be accomplished. We read in Revelation chapter 5 verse 9 that the heavenly creatures praised the Lamb because "with your blood you purchased for God persons from every tribe and language and people and nation." And later in Revelation 7 verses 9–10 John writes, "After this I looked, and there before me was a great multitude that no one could count, from every nation, tribe, people and language, standing before the throne and before the Lamb… And they cried out in a loud voice: 'Salvation belongs to *our* God, who sits on the throne, and to the Lamb.'" (Italics mine)

This is why we should pray for Christians all around the world. This is why we should realize that God is concerned about a lot more than just our little patch here. So in your job, on Wednesday, when you are doing what you do, do you realize that whatever you are doing, you should do for the benefit of others? You should do it for the benefit of Christians, His created and redeemed children, as you show the heart of God.

Our families too will reflect this international nature of Christ's church as people from different ethnic backgrounds come. As a Filipino woman marries an Afro-American man, as Jews marry Gentiles, as Asians date non-Asians, as Americans and non-Americans wed and have children and adopt orphans from other countries, you see how all of this is appropriate in itself by God's ordinance. You don't need Jesus to make this happen. But as appropriate as it is by God's ordinance, it is even more appropriate once you have this new family being created by the Spirit of God. It shows the international character of Christ's church.

It is not just in our families. In our friendships we begin to realize that in Christ we have more in common with others who are redeemed, even if they are from somewhere

IN CHRIST WE HAVE MORE IN COMMON WITH OTHERS WHO ARE REDEEMED, EVEN IF THEY ARE FROM SOMEWHERE ELSE.

else. For example, if you are a Christian who is American, I hope you realize that as much as you have in common with your non-Christian American friends or family, you have got even more in common with your Christian brothers and sisters from Africa and Great Britain and the Caribbean. So we call each other brothers and sisters, not because we are just into some sort of pokey old rural tradition. But it is actually a big theological statement we are making, and that is what we have prayed for when we pray for Christians under oppressive governments, like in Bahrain, Pakistan or Afghanistan.

We pray for Christians, we give our lives to try to get the gospel to all nations, even if that means sacrificing some of the comforts we may know here in the West. That is why some congregations try to give money away to make the gospel of Jesus Christ known around the world. I pray that God will continue to pour out His Spirit on churches to help us sacrifice conveniences as we give ourselves in love to get to know and befriend others who are not just like us.

We pray that even the very relationships that we have in our congregations will provoke the interest of those who come in and visit and know us. Those who come to our homes and see us with friends from the neighborhood and friends from church.

We hope that these relationships will be used to display the gospel to those around us because the Lord has made us Christians together. Christians are international.

JESUS' OWN AGENDA

Interestingly, Jesus could have just said "Give back to Caesar what is Caesar's" and by that clever little answer, pointing out that the coin was owned by Caesar, that would be the end of it. If his image was on it, the sovereign actually owned all the coins they circulated, almost as little bits of his favor. It was a straightforward simple thing to say; just give the coin back to who owns it. And He could have left it at that. They would have had their answer. But once again, Jesus was not operating on their agenda. He had His own agenda.

FINALLY
ACCOUNTABLE
TO GOD

Jesus goes on and what we find is that Christians are finally accountable to God. This is the convicting second half of verse 17, "[Give] to God what is God's." Now, even by saying this, Jesus contradicts what was said on the very denarius they were arguing about. That denarius claimed that the Emperor Tiberius was the son of the divine Augustus, that he himself was a god. Jesus by His statement was clearly distinguishing between Caesar and God. He was clearly saying that Caesar is not God. Jesus' followers would obey the state but they wouldn't worship the state. Christians are good citizens, as we considered previously, but by teaching this, Jesus gives an important additional note, because Christians are finally accountable to God. And because Christians are finally accountable to God, as we see here when it says "[Give] to God what is God's", our duty to earthly authority is limited.

EARTHLY AUTHORITY LIMITED

No earthly kingdom will perfectly reflect the character and authority of God, and we see that when authorities clash. That is when it becomes crystal clear. That is what is going on with the disobedience of Adam and Eve in the Garden of Eden. Adam had authority in the garden, but Adam and Eve didn't use it well. Theirs was the most revolutionary disobedience in all of human history; far more momentous in its consequences than any revolution that has happened since. Everybody else has just been moving around the deckchairs on the *Titanic*. That one changed everything. They were the revolutionaries of all revolutionaries. Since then, this pattern of rebelling against God's authority has continued and it is sadly well represented in the scriptures by a number of pagan rulers. Pick just one example from Exodus 5 verse 2: "Pharaoh said, 'Who is the Lord, that I should obey him and let Israel go? I do not know the Lord and I will not let Israel go.'"

Well! Things didn't turn out quite as he thought they would. Pharaoh, we have to understand, had legitimate authority. He was a legitimate ruler of Egypt, but his authority was being abused as he opposed God Himself, and that is why we end up with the story again and again in the Old Testament of the human oppression that goes on through government. That is why the psalmist can write in Psalm 119 verse 134, "Redeem me from human oppression, that I may obey your precepts." Not all authority is used for good, though authority in its very essence is good by its very nature. Authority is not always used for good in a fallen world.

In the New Testament, we see this with Jesus' own disciples, after His ascension in Acts chapter 4, the Sanhedrin ordered Peter and John not to speak or preach anymore in the name of Jesus of Nazareth and in Acts chapter 4 verse 19 Peter and John responded "Which is right in God's eyes: to listen to you, or to him? You be the judges!" And then in the next chapter, when in fact they had disobeyed the instruction and are again brought in before the Sanhedrin, and are again ordered not to do this, Acts chapter 5 verse 29 says, "Peter and the other apostles replied, 'We must obey God rather than human beings!'"

How do we know when our will conflicts with God or His will? How do we know when government does something that is wrong? How do we know that it is wrong? Well, we learn in the Bible that God is never wrong but human governments do err, just like in these examples I have just given you from the book of Acts. That means that we necessarily have to leave some space for civil disobedience when an authority commands something that is morally wrong. As a pastor with a congregation, I would tell them, you should not obey the government if the government tells you to do something that God has told you not to do. You should not obey, because by obeying you would be obeying a true but lower authority and contravening something which the highest authority, God Himself, has told us, and that would be morally wrong.

Our congregation in Washington DC was begun in 1878 with 18 articles about what we believe to be true. Article 16 says this, "We believe that Civil Government is of Divine Appointment, for the interests and good order of human society; that magistrates are to be prayed for, conscientiously honored and obeyed." And you think, good, that is a good biblical statement, but that's not all. There is one last phrase, "Except only in things opposed to the will of our Lord Jesus Christ, who is the only Lord of the conscience and the Prince of the kings of the earth."

We understand there is a legitimate role for government and we are thankful for it, and we understand that earthly governments are not the ultimate authority. So if Romans 13 tells us about the good of the state, Revelation 13 gives us a picture of what happens when the state clashes with God and opposes God and persecutes Christians. We must not be surprised by that. Jesus had already told His disciples in Mark 8:34, "Whoever wants to be my disciple must deny themselves and take up their cross and follow me." Crucifixion was an action of the state. To follow Jesus means to imperil yourself in a fallen world and He was about to teach them in John 15:20, "Remember what I told you: 'A servant is not greater than his master.' If they persecuted me, they will persecute you also."

The Bible is clear that all people are made in the image of God and that people are fallen and guilty before God. And every single one of us will have to give account ultimately not to the government of the district of Columbia, not to the government of the UK or whatever country you come from, we will all of us, whether or not you believe in God, one day give account to the one true living God who created us and who will judge us.

If your conscience is alive at all, you know you have got things to answer for, you have not always done what is right and the God who really is there is perfectly holy, perfectly good, perfectly loving, perfectly true, perfectly reliable and trustworthy, He is the one that we have to give account to. I love what my friend Vijay Menon says: "All religions lead to God, no question about that. All empty out there right in front of the judgment seat of God. But there is only one religion that has a Savior. Jesus Christ is the Savior you need."

THERE IS ONLY ONE RELIGION THAT HAS A SAVIOR. JESUS CHRIST IS THE SAVIOR YOU NEED.

That is why Jesus came. This is one of the problems with referring to any country as a Christian nation. Just because the principles of Christianity clearly influenced a nation's founders, and they often did, even if the Supreme Court or judicial system of a country has recognized the long history of and significant influence of Christianity, that does not mean that most citizens are Christians, or that a Christian world view dominates our public polls, or government.

Augustine understood these complexities when he wrote in his book *The City of God* about how we as Christians find ourselves simultaneously being citizens of two cities. We are a part of the city of man and the city of God at the same time; citizens of both. The legal establishment of Christianity in many nations centuries after the apostles reflected an already distorted understanding of the gospel, and led to terrible confusions as the church wielded the sword in religious wars and inquisitions. And I think we are tempted to similar confusions today.

Take 2 Chronicles 7:14. "If my people, who are called by my name, will humble themselves and pray and seek my face and turn from their wicked ways, then I will hear from heaven, and I will forgive their sin and will heal their land." It is part of the inerrant Word of God but I think Christians' identification of their land, whatever it is, with Israel and 2 Chronicles 7:14 is very well intended but is confusing. There are no specific promises in the Bible like that for any nation state in the world today, though it is true we should always repent and God may in His mercy bless our land! That is really over to Him.

PASSING POWER

Even if we have leaders who are Christians, the authority of our government will never be used perfectly. We pray for our leaders. We pray for the nations that we would be good stewards of all the blessings that God has undisputedly given us in the West, and we try to stay on guard against the allure of worldly power. We know that it isn't perfect and that this worldly power will vanish. I recount Wesley's words: "I was in the robe chamber adjoining to the House of Lords when the King put on his robes. His brow was much furrowed with age and quite crowded with care. And is this all the world can give even to a King? All the grandeur it can afford? A blanket of ermine around his shoulders so heavy and cumbersome he can scarce move under it! A huge heap of borrowed hair, with a few plates of gold and glittering stones upon his head. Alas, what a bauble is human greatness! And even this will not endure!"[ii]

Your work is important because of your relationship to God, because of what God calls you to do, not because of your earthly boss. Your earthly boss is passing and temporary, but there is a heavenly master who sees how you work and what you do and it is to Him that you are to do everything that you do. For His sake and for His glory and for His honor. We should certainly take from Jesus' second phrase here, "[Give] to God what is God's", a reminder that we should obey God rather than any boss we may ever have that would tell us to do something wrong. And that includes the state. So should we obey the state when it tells us that we can't spank a child, but you can abort an infant? The state has important authority, but it is limited wherever it conflicts with God's authority.

OUR DUTY TO GOD

Questions of how and when we should disobey the state should be thought through very carefully and with study of Scripture, reflection, prayer and counsel. But in a fallen world we can never rule such action necessarily wrong. We can pray for wisdom in political matters, but we must allow for differences in partisanship. We resist identifying the gospel with any particular nation or any political party, and we look forward to the day when we are done with all of that and God again rules us immediately, and fallible earthly authority is no more.

Though our duty to earthly authority is limited, our duty to God is comprehensive. Jesus says, "[Give] to God what is God's." Praise God earthly governments don't have the last say, and I don't mean that offensively to any one nation. I am just saying that is the way it is since the Fall. In a fallen world, legal is not the same thing as moral. Illegal is not necessarily the same thing as immoral and so earthly authority must humbly remember that it is not the ultimate power. Remember that Jesus said in Matthew

> THOUGH OUR DUTY TO EARTHLY AUTHORITY IS LIMITED, OUR DUTY TO GOD IS COMPREHENSIVE.

28 verse 18 that He had "All authority in heaven and on earth". In just a few verses in Mark chapter 12 and verse 30 he is going to go on to tell them to love the Lord with all that you are and have. Jesus wasn't a revolutionary fundamentally against Rome. He was a much more radical revolutionary, leading a revolt against the dominion of sin and death. That was the revolution he was starting.

WE ARE HIS

You see, when Jesus points out His ownership of that which bears Caesar's image, He is implying God's ownership of all of us because we bear God's image. We are His. Therefore you give that coin back to Caesar but you give yourself to God. Any obligation we have to the state, is a part of our larger responsibility to God with our whole lives because we are part of His creation and we will be judged by Him, not least because we Christians have been created again by Him and bought back with a price.

> WE BEAR GOD'S IMAGE. WE ARE HIS. THEREFORE YOU GIVE THAT COIN BACK TO CAESAR BUT YOU GIVE YOURSELF TO GOD.

So all authority is God's and it belongs to Jesus. We have seen that. Evil spirits and the winds and the waves obey Him. He is the Son of God and it is our duty now to obey Him entirely. Look at Mark 12 verse 17, this was a stinging indictment against human beings whose ears were hearing what Jesus said. Look at that parable He has just told in verses 1 to 12.

Jesus then began to speak to them in parables: "A man planted a vineyard. He put a wall around it, dug a pit for the winepress and built a watchtower. Then he rented the vineyard to some farmers and moved to another place. ² At harvest time he sent a servant to the tenants to collect from them some of the fruit of the vineyard. ³ But they seized him, beat him and sent him away empty-handed. ⁴ Then he sent another servant to them; they struck this man on the head and treated him shamefully. ⁵ He sent still another, and that one they killed. He sent many others; some of them they beat, others they killed.

⁶ "He had one left to send, a son, whom he loved. He sent him last of all, saying, 'They will respect my son.'

⁷ "But the tenants said to one another, 'This is the heir. Come, let's kill him, and the inheritance will be ours.' 8 So they took him and killed him, and threw him out of the vineyard.

⁹ "What then will the owner of the vineyard do? He will come and kill those tenants and give the vineyard to others. ¹⁰ Haven't you read this passage of Scripture:

"'The stone the builders rejected

   has become the cornerstone;

¹¹ the Lord has done this,

   and it is marvelous in our eyes'?"

¹² Then the chief priests, the teachers of the law and the elders looked for a way to arrest him because they knew he had spoken the parable against them. But they were afraid of the crowd; so they left him and went away.

Jesus' listeners were the wicked tenants. They owed God all that they had. Jesus the Son was there, and they as the tenants in the parable were rejecting Him by the way they were questioning Him. Jesus the Son has come to collect what is due, and guess what is due? You are! That is what He was saying to those people who were hearing Him that day and they were refusing to pay. What happened in the story? He says in verse 9, "What then will the owner of the vineyard do? He will come and kill those tenants and give the vineyard to others."

That evening Jesus' disciples are going to notice the sheer size and magnificence of the temple, and He is going to say that not one stone is going to be left standing. He is going to talk in Mark chapter 13 about how God is going to judge because of the rejection of His Messiah. But, this is also an indictment against each one of us, because we are all made in God's image. Every one of us owes God everything we have and are. And so this should drive us to Christ as our Savior.

God sent Christ into the world to live a life of complete reliance on His heavenly Father, trusting Him at every point, trusting His authority. Then He died the death that He died as a sacrifice and as a substitute for all of us who have ever rebelled against God, and that is every single one of us. And God raised Jesus from the dead to show that He accepted the sacrifice, and He pours out His Spirit and gives new life. He gives forgiveness for our sins. He gives us reconciliation to God for everyone who will repent of their sins and turn and trust in Christ alone for salvation.

That is what you should do today if you have not already done so. That is how you respond to this command to give to God what is God's. Pay your taxes but even more, trust in Christ. That is the point of this verse. Trust in the one who can exonerate you and reconcile you to God.

The fact that we should give to God what is God's means that we should also look to include God in every area of our life. Paul said in Colossians 3 verse 17, "whatever you do, whether in word or deed, do it all in the name of the Lord Jesus, giving thanks to God the Father through him."

HOUR BY HOUR

Your whole life, every day, every hour is being offered to God as part of your worship to Him. So that hour you spend doing IT work, that hour you spend as a lawyer, that hour you spend preparing responsibly for something coming up, that hour you spend caring for your wife, that hour you spend caring for your husband or your family, that hour you spend caring for your friends or preparing a report, you realize that all of that is meant to be to God's glory. Every single one of those hours.

Husbands, the way you use authority in your wife's life is meant to reflect God's own authority. Parents, when you use your authority in your children's lives you are teaching them what God is like. In whatever position you have in authority, you are reflecting the truth about God. You are showing up Satan as a deceiver and you are exposing his slanders against God as lies. God is worthy of being trusted entirely. He is worthy of being obeyed and followed implicitly.

Pray for preachers of God's Word too that we would understand and apply the Bible well. We want to teach the Word and we want to live in such a way that we instruct our hearers in all of life. We want to explain so that you can say what Hebrews 13 verse 7 says of us "Remember your leaders, who spoke the word of God to you. Consider the outcome of their way of life and imitate their faith." Because God is to be the Lord of every area of our lives. When Abraham Kuyper opened the free university of Amsterdam about 100 years ago, he gave a speech in which he famously said, "There is not a square inch in the whole domain of our human existence over which Christ, who is sovereign over all, does not cry, 'Mine'."

Our duty to God is comprehensive. Give to God what is God's and everything is God's. Give who you are to Him.

A VISION FOR OUR HEARTS

So, does Christianity have a vision for the state and society as a whole? Or is Christianity, as my Muslim friend implied, so heavenly minded that it is of no earthly good? I think visions like the one my friend had for the state are way too shallow. Jesus Christ comes to do something much deeper than any social revolutionary has ever done or ever been able to do. He has come to actually change our whole hearts. To change our natures. The Bible shows us that God has a wonderful vision for His world. We have all rejected that vision and yet, even after that rejection, God in His amazing mercy and love continues to pursue us. Jesus Christ, God's own Son, stood teaching the very people that would, a few days' later, seek His life, arrest Him, beat Him and have Him put to death.

> JESUS CHRIST, GOD'S OWN SON, STOOD TEACHING THE VERY PEOPLE THAT WOULD, A FEW DAYS' LATER, SEEK HIS LIFE, ARREST HIM, BEAT HIM AND HAVE HIM PUT TO DEATH.

I know that there are Marxist and Muslim utopian visions for our world. There are secular visions too, but none of these visions sufficiently takes into account the things the Bible teaches about every human being. About our being made in God's image, about God's goodness, about His love, His holiness. Utopian visions of politics or of nations always lead to tragedy. They always lead to tyranny and despotism and terrible distortions of God's will.

It is the truth of Christianity that tells us about God being holy and loving and our being made in God's image and yet fallen. God's provisions and promises for us in crisis lead us to sufficiently respect the fallen governments of the world, and yet, give us hope to endure them and to work and hope for something infinitely better.

God gives us the peace which comes with such hope and the strength to get up and face another day, to continue following Jesus, until He brings us home, where we will never, never need to worry about being or obeying Caesar again. There will be no mediating authorities. So, go ahead and give to Caesar what is Caesar's but then give to God what is God's and remember you belong to God, all of you.

END NOTES

i David Brooks, The Gospel of Wealth, *The New York Times* 6 September 2010

www.nytimes.com/2010/09/07/opinion/07brooks.html?_r=0

ii Wesley, *Inspiration 3*, p. 119

10Publishing is the publishing house of 10ofThose. It is committed to producing quality Christian resources that are biblical and accessible.

www.10ofthose.com is where all our titles are available. They are all priced so that the more you buy the cheaper they get.

For information contact: sales@10ofthose.com or check out our website: www.10ofthose.com